SUPER BOWL

DENVER BRONCOS

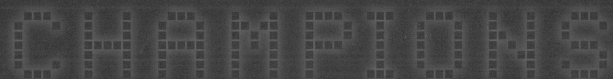

CHAMPIONS

SUPER BOWL

Published by Creative Education
123 South Broad Street
Mankato, Minnesota 56001
Creative Education is an imprint of The Creative Company.

DESIGN AND PRODUCTION BY **EVANSDAY DESIGN**

LIBRARY OF CONGRESS CATALOGING-IN-PUBLICATION DATA

LeBoutillier, Nate.
Denver Broncos / by Nate LeBoutillier.
p. cm. — (Super Bowl champions)
Includes index.
ISBN 1-58341-383-9
1. Denver Broncos (Football team)—Juvenile literature. I. Title. II. Series.
GV956.D37L43 2005
796.332'64'0978883—dc22   2005048357

First edition

9 8 7 6 5 4 3 2 1

COVER PHOTO: cornerback Champ Bailey

PHOTOGRAPHS BY
AP/Wide World Photos, Corbis (Bettmann, Steve Boyle/NewSport, Paul Spinelli, Rick Wilking/Reuters), Getty Images (Brian Bahr, Tim DeFrisco/Allsport),
SportsChrome USA

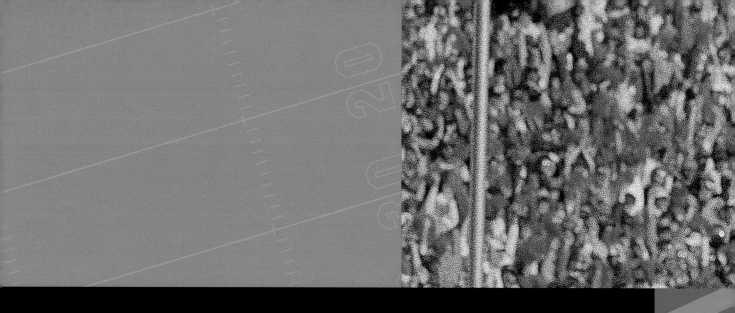

THE BRONCOS are a professional football team in the National Football League (NFL). They play in Denver, Colorado. Denver is called "The Mile High City." It is in the Rocky Mountains. Sometimes the Broncos play in cold weather.

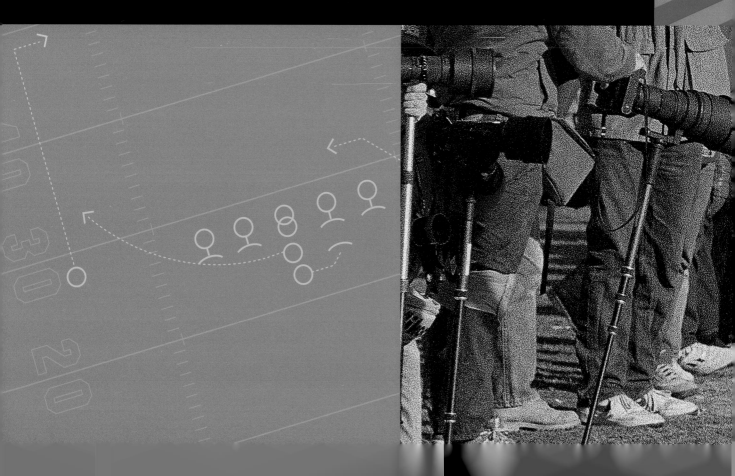

THE BRONCOS play in a stadium called INVESCO Field at Mile High. A bronco is a kind of rodeo horse. The Broncos' helmets are blue with a bronco's head on the side. Their uniforms are orange, blue, and white. The Broncos play many games against teams called the Chargers, Chiefs, and Raiders.

THE BRONCOS played their first season in 1960. They beat the Boston Patriots 13–10 to win their very first game. It was an exciting start!

FLOYD LITTLE was the Broncos' first great player. He was a running back who was very strong and fast. He played for nine seasons in Denver.

Floyd Little was not very tall, but he was a good jumper ^

Red Miller coached Denver during some exciting seasons ^

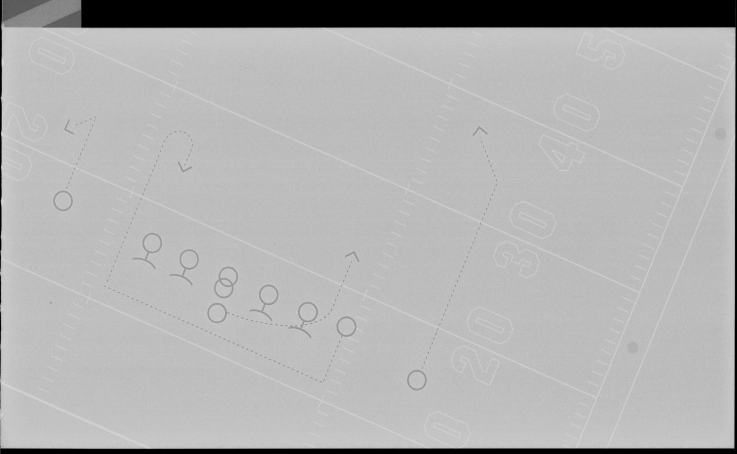

IN 1977, the Broncos had some new players and a new coach named Red Miller. They got all the way to the Super Bowl. Even though the Broncos lost, it was an exciting time that fans called "Broncomania."

QUARTERBACK John Elway is the only Broncos player in the NFL Hall of Fame. Fans called him "The Comeback Kid." He liked to lead the Broncos to victory in the last minute of games.

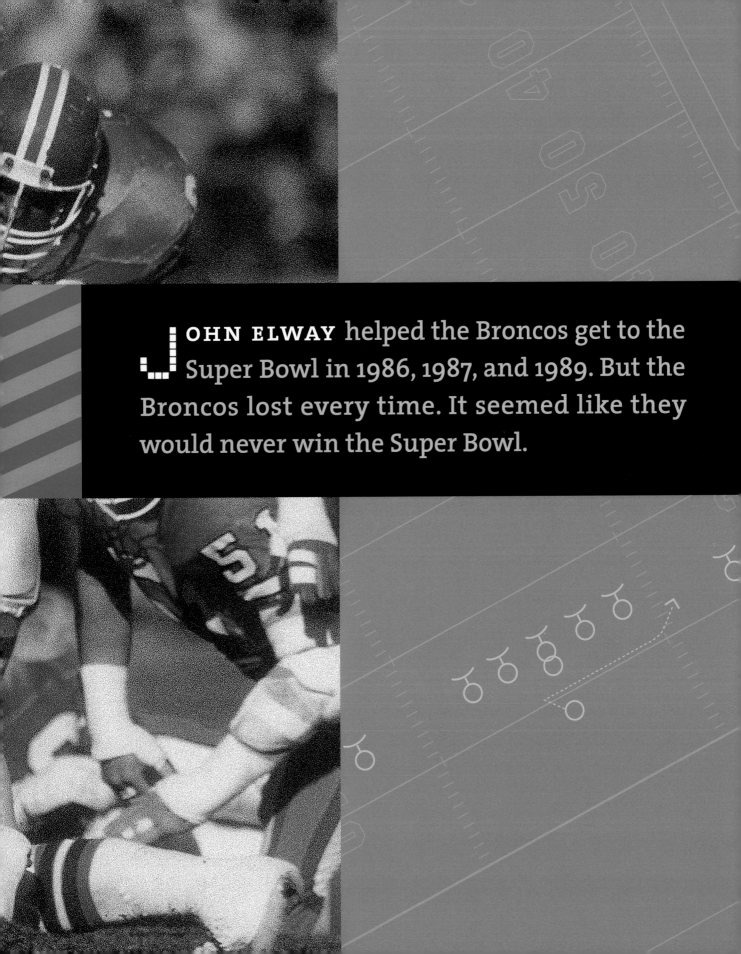

JOHN ELWAY helped the Broncos get to the Super Bowl in 1986, 1987, and 1989. But the Broncos lost every time. It seemed like they would never win the Super Bowl.

IN 1997, the Broncos had a fast running back named Terrell Davis. He helped John Elway and the Broncos get to the Super Bowl again. This time, they beat the Green Bay Packers to become world champions. The Broncos won the Super Bowl the next year, too!

TODAY, THE Broncos have a new quarterback named Jake Plummer. Fans call him "Jake the Snake." They hope he will help the Broncos get back to the Super Bowl soon.

Hall of Fame
a club that only the best NFL players and coaches
get to join

National Football League (NFL)
a group of football teams that play against each other;
there are 32 teams in the NFL today

professional
a person or team that gets paid to play or work

rodeo
an event where cowboys show off their riding and
roping skills

Team colors
Orange, blue, and white

Home stadium
INVESCO Field at Mile High (76,125 seats)

Conference/Division
American Football Conference (AFC), West Division

First season
1960

Super Bowl wins
1997 (beat Green Bay Packers 31–24)
1998 (beat Atlanta Falcons 34–19)

Training camp location
Englewood, Colorado

Broncos Web site for kids
http://www.denverbroncos.com/page.php?id=611

NFL Web site for kids
http://www.playfootball.com

INDEX